Editor
Sara Connolly

Editor in Chief
Karen J. Goldfluss, M.S. Ed.

Illustrator
Clint McKnight

Cover Artist
Diem Pascarella

Art Coordinator
Renée Mc Elwee

Imaging
James Edward Grace
Craig Gunnell

Publisher
Mary D. Smith, M.S. Ed.

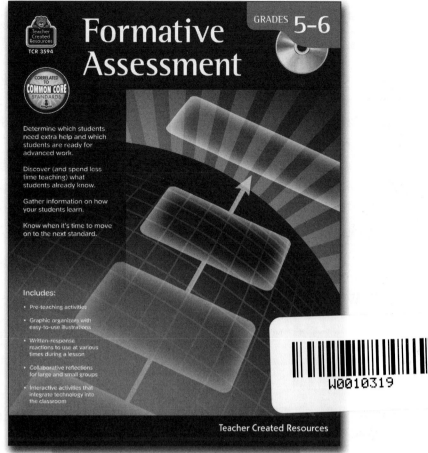

Author
Susan Mackey Collins, M.Ed.

For correlations to the Common Core State Standards, see page 4 or visit **http://www.teachercreated.com/standards.**

Teacher Created Resources
6421 Industry Way
Westminster, CA 92683
www.teachercreated.com

ISBN: 978-1-4206-3594-2

© 2014 Teacher Created Resources
Made in U.S.A.

Table of Contents

Introduction

Good assessment is vital to effective instruction. *Formative Assessment (Grades 5–6)* provides clear and effective resources to use for classroom formative assessments. Instructors in all subject areas must vary their methods of assessment to be sure each student clearly understands the standards being taught. This is where successful formative assessment is a must in any discipline.

Formative assessment provides feedback on a student's understanding of the concept being taught. The root word "form" in "formative" reminds the educator that the assessment method should be used to help *form* the lesson or skill being taught; the formative assessment can help the teacher decide if a student needs more instruction with a specific standard or has mastered the skill being taught and is ready to move on to something new.

Assessment that is formative should be used daily and provide classroom practice over the standard being taught. Methods of assessment can and should vary to ensure the teacher is meeting the differentiated learning styles of all students. Teachers should use formative assessment to ensure all students are successful with a specific standard before students are given a summative or graded assessment. Using formative assessment daily can also provide evidence that some students in the classroom are ready to move on to more advanced work with a specific standard. The results of formative assessment allow those students who are skilled in a specific area to be able to continue their own individual progress rather than waiting on other students to reach a specific goal.

This book is divided into five sections for quick and easy reference:

- Pre-Teaching: formative assessment activities to use before a lesson
- Graphic Organizers: formative assessment organizers with easy-to-use illustrations
- Written Response: formative assessment reactions to use during various times during the lesson
- Collaborative Reflections: formative assessment activities to use with both small and large groups
- Technology and Interactive Assessment: formative assessment activities that integrate technology into the classroom

Formative assessment is a necessary tool to help student achievement improve in all subjects and at all levels of learning.

Common Core Standards and Formative Assessment

Formative Assessment (Grades 5–6) is designed to be a teaching tool that helps implement formative assessment while teaching Common Core standards. Formative assessment is a vital part of making sure students are successful with Common Core standards. Since the standards provide a clear map for teaching literacy skills in all content areas, it is vital that all content areas be prepared to use formative assessments.

No matter how well a standard is written, if a student is not mastering the standard, he or she will not be successful and able to move on to the next higher level of learning. Good formative assessment allows a teacher to know what needs to happen next in the classroom and to meet the diversity of learning styles of each individual student. Good formative assessment also allows the student to be proactive in knowing where his or her weakness or strengths are in a particular standard. Self-assessment is key to formative assessment.

Common Core State Standards

Each activity in this book meets one or more of the following Common Core State Standards © Copyright 2010. National Governors Association Center for Best Practices and Council of Chief State School Officers. All rights reserved. For more information about the Common Core State Standards, go to **http://www.corestandards.org** or **http://www.teachercreated.com/standards/**.

Writing Standards	
Text Types and Purposes	
ELA-Literacy.W.5.1	Write opinion pieces on topics or texts, supporting a point of view with reasons and information.
ELA-Literacy.W.6.1	Write arguments to support claims with clear reasons and relevant evidence.
ELA-Literacy.W.5.2	Write informative/explanatory texts to examine a topic and convey ideas and information clearly.
ELA-Literacy.W.6.2	Write informative/explanatory texts to examine a topic and convey ideas, concepts, and information through the selection, organization, and analysis of relevant content.
ELA-Literacy.W.5.3	Write narratives to develop real or imagined experiences or events using effective technique, descriptive details, and clear event sequences.
ELA-Literacy.W.6.3	Write narratives to develop real or imagined experiences or events using effective technique, relevant descriptive details, and well-structured event sequences.
Production and Distribution of Writing	
ELA-Literacy.W.5.6	With some guidance and support from adults, use technology, including the Internet, to produce and publish writing as well as to interact and collaborate with others; demonstrate sufficient command of keyboarding skills to type a minimum of two pages in a single sitting.
ELA-Literacy.W.6.6	Use technology, including the Internet, to produce and publish writing as well as to interact and collaborate with others; demonstrate sufficient command of keyboarding skills to type a minimum of three pages in a single sitting.
Speaking & Listening Standards	
Comprehension and Collaboration	
ELA-Literacy.SL.5.1	Engage effectively in a range of collaborative discussions (one-on-one, in groups, and teacher-led) with diverse partners on grade 5 topics and texts, building on others' ideas and expressing their own clearly.
ELA-Literacy.SL.5.2	Summarize a written text read aloud or information presented in diverse media and formats, including visually, quantitatively, and orally.
ELA-Literacy.SL.6.1	Engage effectively in a range of collaborative discussions (one-on-one, in groups, and teacher-led) with diverse partners on grade 6 topics, texts, and issues, building on others' ideas and expressing their own clearly.
ELA-Literacy.SL.6.2	Interpret information presented in diverse media and formats (e.g., visually, quantitatively, orally) and explain how it contributes to a topic, text, or issue under study.
Language Standards	
Vocabulary Acquisition and Use	
ELA-Literacy.L.5.4	Determine or clarify the meaning of unknown and multiple-meaning words and phrases based on grade 5 reading and content, choosing flexibly from a range of strategies.
ELA-Literacy.L.6.4	Determine or clarify the meaning of unknown and multiple-meaning words and phrases based on grade 6 reading and content, choosing flexibly from a range of strategies.

Eight Great Ways to Use Formative Assessment

Use pre-assessment formative activities before beginning a unit. Assess where your class is as a whole. Use this information to decide where to begin and to see who might need extra help and who might be ready for advanced work. Look at each activity carefully and change or add to any idea before making copies for the class. This will ensure the assessment will work best for each situation. This is true for all types of formative assessments.

Use pre-assessment formative activities to discover students who might need instruction outside the time in the regular classroom. Find time to meet with these students before starting a new unit or send home enrichment activities the student can do to help prepare him or her for the new standard.

Use the formative assessment activities to help form your lesson plans. Do not spend time teaching what your students already know; use the formative assessment activities to help you see which standards need the most time.

Use formative assessment outcomes that reflect understanding of a standard as rewards. Create incentive charts for students. Give incentives or stickers to students who do well on the assessments. Have an agreed-upon reward as individual students complete their charts.

Use formative assessment to gather information about your students. Find out how much your students remember from a previous year or even a previous unit to help you plan your lessons.

Use formative assessment for participation grades, not completion grades. Formative assessments show the teacher what a student knows at a certain point in the lesson; summative assessments show what a student knows at the end of the instruction.

Use formative assessment to gather information about the various learning styles of the students in the classroom. Use the information to help create differentiated instruction so that all the students can be successful while still adding rigor to the lesson.

Use formative assessment to know when it is time to give a summative or graded assessment. Mastery of formative assessments gives the teacher a clear understanding of when to move to the next standard.

Name: _____

You're on the Clock

Directions: Listen carefully as the teacher says the topic of today's lesson. You will have three minutes to write or illustrate anything you already know about today's lesson. Write in the space inside the clock to record your thoughts.

If you do not already know anything about today's topic, draw three question marks inside the clock.

Today's topic is _____.

Something extra: When people are "on the clock," they are considered to be working. After hearing today's lesson, how could the skill(s) that were presented be used outside of school or at someone's place of work? On the back of this page, write a well-developed paragraph explaining your answer.

Name: _____

Three Wishes

Materials needed: scissors, tape, teacher-prepared section for completed genie bottles

Directions: Listen carefully as the teacher says the topic of today's lesson.

Now use the genie bottles below to write down one or both of the following:

1. Any wish for information you have about the topic

2. Anything you wish the teacher realized you already knew about the topic

Once you have written your wishes, cut out the bottles and use tape to stick them in the area of the room the teacher has prepared. The teacher will use the wishes to help guide the lesson.

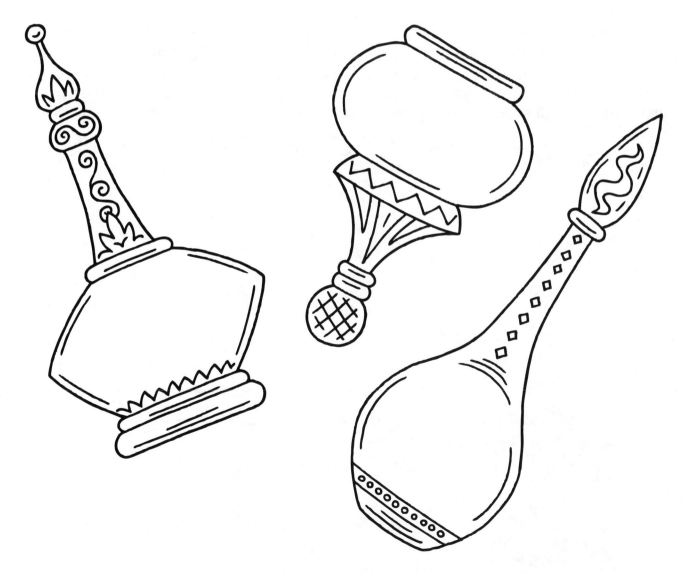

Name: _____

My Thoughts

For today's assessment, you will be asked to illustrate or write everything you know about a topic before your teacher gives you any instruction. Look at the example to help you understand the directions that follow.

> **Example:** Today's topic is metric measurements.
>
> You aren't sure what the measurements are, but you know the cola your family buys is in a two-liter bottle, which you think has something to do with metrics, so you draw a picture of a two-liter bottle.

Directions: Listen carefully as the teacher says the topic of today's lesson. Write the topic on the line:

_____ .

Think about everything you might already know about today's topic. Use the space below to write or illustrate what you already know. You can write down ideas, words, or phrases, or give examples about the topic. If you cannot think of anything you already know about the topic, make a guess, and write or illustrate something you think might be related to today's topic.

Name: _____

Write Now

Directions: Answer each question .

1. What is the topic of today's lesson? _____

2. If I could ask one question before class begins that is related to the topic, I would ask the

   following question: _____

3. Look at the chart below. Color in the single star that corresponds with your thoughts
   about today's topic.

I know a lot about this topic.	I know something about this topic.	I know little about this topic.	I know I have never heard about this topic.
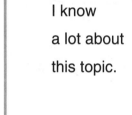		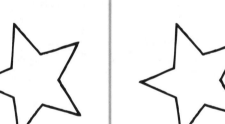	

4. Does today's topic seem similar to anything else you have studied? _____

   If you answered *yes*, explain your answer. _____

   _____

   If you answered *no*, make a prediction about why this is an important topic the class
   needs to learn.

   _____

5. Ask someone else in the classroom what he or she knows about today's topic. Write the
   answer you are given on the following lines. Use the back of the page if you need more
   space.

   _____

   _____

Name: _____

Definitions

Materials needed: print or electronic dictionary

Directions: Listen carefully as the teacher says the topic of today's lesson. Write the topic on the line that follows:

_____

Look at the open dictionary drawn below. On page 1, write a definition for today's topic. Use your own words to create your definition. If you are unsure about the topic, write a definition for the word "unsure."

Next, use a dictionary to look up the important or "key" word or words listed in today's lesson topic. Write the word or words on page 2 of the dictionary picture. Write the dictionary definitions you have found out beside the word(s).

Compare what you have written on Page 1 to what is written on Page 2. Circle or highlight any similarities.

Use any remaining space to take notes during today's lesson.

Name: _____

Say It With Words and Pictures

Listen carefully as the teacher states the topic of the lesson.

Write the topic on the line: _____

Follow the remaining directions to complete the assessment.

Part 1

Directions: Think about today's topic. In the box below, write down anything you already know about the topic. If you do not have any previous knowledge about the topic, list two places where you might learn more about the topic.

_____

_____

_____

_____

_____

Part 2

Directions: Illustrate what you already know about the topic. The illustration can include graphs, pictures, equations, etc. If you do not have any previous knowledge about the topic, draw a picture of one of the sources you listed above where someone could find more information about the topic.

Name: _____

Before You Begin

Directions: Write a short answer for each question.

1. What is the topic, lesson, or standard being taught?

_____

2. How might this be important to anyone outside of school?

_____

3. Look at the lesson topic and write one fact you believe might be true about today's topic.

_____

_____

4. Could this topic be important in any subject other than this class? Explain your answer.

_____

_____

5. If you could ask the teacher any question about the topic before you begin the lesson, what would you ask?

_____

_____

6. Make a prediction: After the lesson, how will the teacher assess the information to see if everyone in the class understands the skill(s)?

_____

_____

_____

Name: _____

Half Empty? Half Full?

Listen carefully as the teacher states the topic or standard to be covered during today's lesson.

Part 1

Directions: Write the topic of today's lesson underneath the picture of the glass. Use your pencil to shade in the straw to show how much you already know about today's lesson.

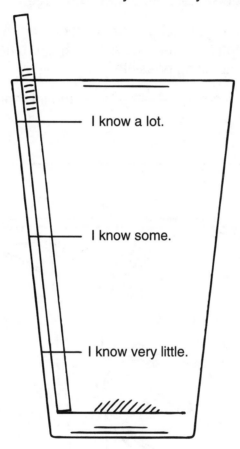

— I know a lot.

— I know some.

— I know very little.

Today's topic: _____

• •

Part 2

Directions: Think about any type of juice or soda. Compare today's topic to the drink. On the back of the page, explain how the topic reminds you of this drink.

Example: The topic of fractions reminds me of orange juice because the original fruit is eaten in small fractions or parts, and it is refreshing to drink, and this is a refreshing topic because we are learning something new. Also, I drink orange juice at breakfast with my waffles, and each indention in the waffle represents a fraction of the total part.

Name: _____

Fill Up the Cart

Materials needed: scissors, glue, one copy of page 15 for each student.

Directions: With the teacher's help, divide into groups of three to four students.

Write the lesson topic or standard on the front of the shopping-cart sign on page 15. *Hint:* Each person in the group must complete his or her own page.

Discuss with the group everything you already know about the topic. Write facts about the topic on the food items at the bottom. Cut out each item and glue each one into the shopping cart. Try to complete as many items as possible.

Note: Members in the group can have the same facts and information in each of their carts. Use the example below to help you get started.

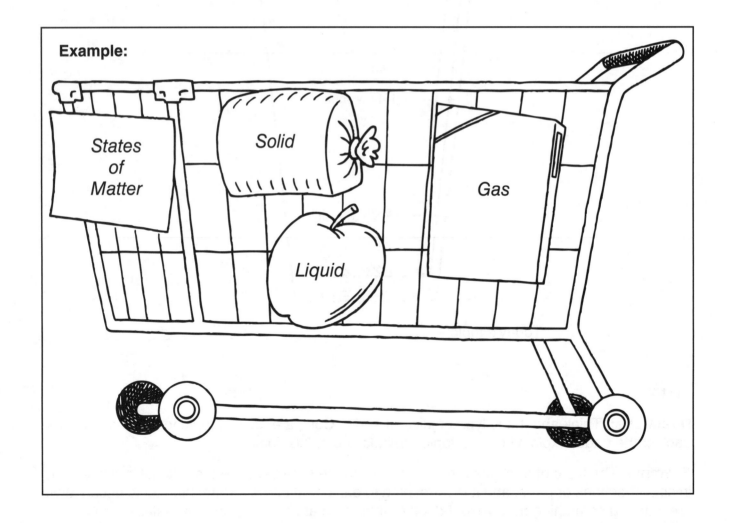

Example:

States of Matter

Solid

Liquid

Gas

Name: _____

Fill Up the Cart *(cont.)*

Directions: Write facts about the lesson topic on the food items below. Cut out the items and glue each one inside the shopping cart. Write the topic of today's lesson on the sign on the cart.

Name: _____

Higher Knowledge

Materials needed: yellow, orange, and blue crayons

Directions: Complete the hot air balloon by following each direction.

1. Write the standard or topic of today's lesson on the basket of the hot air balloon.

2. Write one question you have about today's topic in the left panel. Color the panel yellow.

3. Write one fact you learned about today's topic in the middle panel. Color the panel orange.

4. Design or illustration something you learned during today's lesson about the topic in the right panel. Color the panel blue.

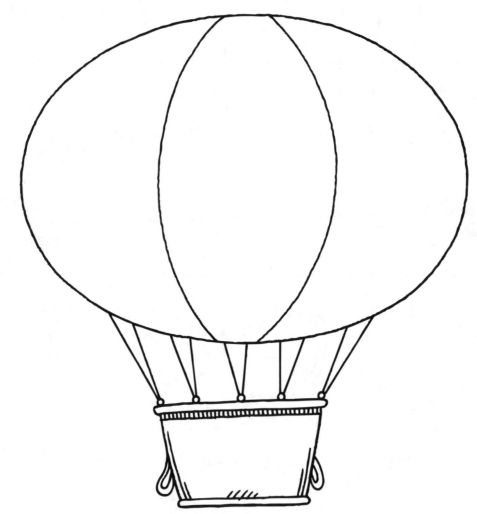

Something extra: Draw three clouds around the hot air balloon. Inside each cloud, write questions you have about the lesson and/or more facts you learned during the lesson.

Name: _____

Building Blocks

The new things one learns are building blocks for understanding other topics or lessons. For example, a student might learn about quotation marks so he or she can later write dialogue for a narrative.

Directions: Write the topic of standard from today's lesson on the bottom block. Complete the tower by answering each question.

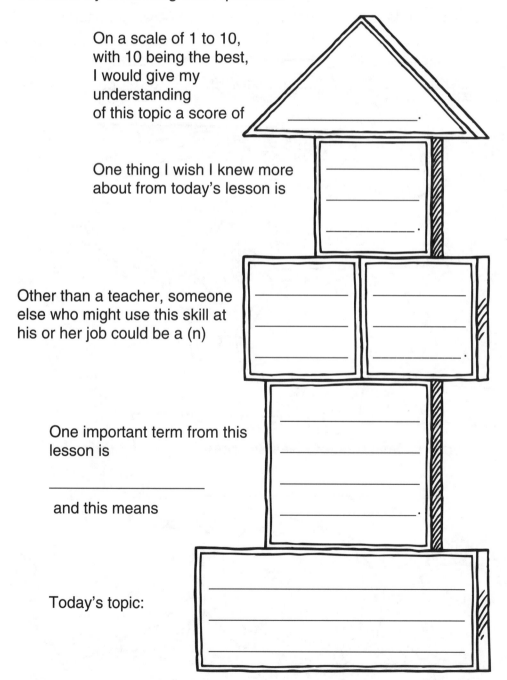

On a scale of 1 to 10, with 10 being the best, I would give my understanding of this topic a score of _____.

One thing I wish I knew more about from today's lesson is _____.

Other than a teacher, someone else who might use this skill at his or her job could be a (n) _____.

One important term from this lesson is

_____

and this means _____.

Today's topic: _____

Name: _____

A Real Treasure

Materials needed: yellow and red crayons

Directions: Write the topic or standard from today's lesson on the treasure trunk.

Write "gems of information" you learned from today's lesson on at least four of the stones in the treasure trunk. Color these stones yellow.

Write any questions you have about today's lesson on any of the other pieces of treasure. Color these pieces red.

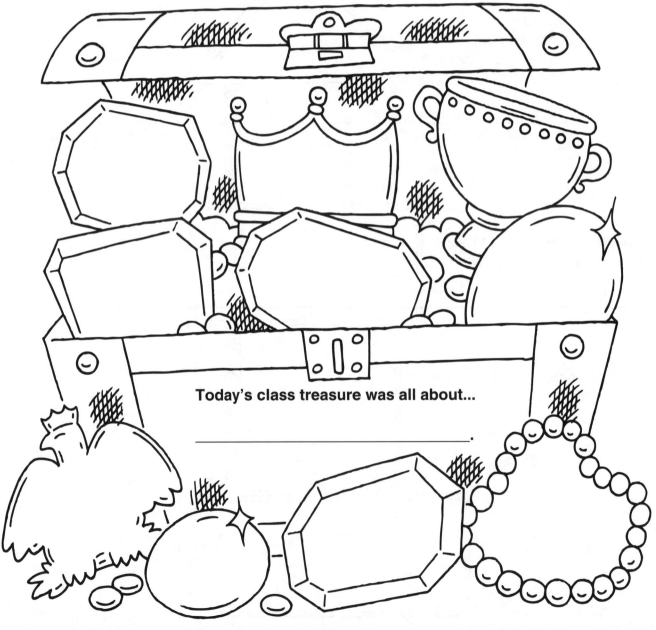

Today's class treasure was all about...

_____.

Name: _____

I Learned "A Bunch"

Lots of things come in "bunches," and hopefully during the lesson you learned a bunch of new things! How much is a bunch? It all depends on what it is...but for this lesson, a bunch is two or more.

Use the graphic organizer below to help show off everything you know about today's topic.

Directions: Complete the directions for each picture. All writing should be done on and next to the illustrations.

a. Write a bunch of facts about the lesson.

b. Write a bunch of ways you might use today's lesson outside of this class.

c. Write a bunch of questions you might ask someone on a quiz about today's lesson.

d. Write a bunch of adjectives that describe today's topic.

Name: _____

All-in-One Setting

Directions: Use the place setting below and the directions that are given to write about today's lesson.

a. On the fork, write one thing you already knew about the topic before the lesson began.

b. On the center of the plate, write the topic of the lesson.

c. On the saucer, write one question you still have about today's topic.

d. On the knife, write a vocabulary word from the lesson and its definition.

e. On the spoon, draw a face with a smile if you understand today's lesson. Leave it blank if you do not.

Name: _____

Charged Up and Ready to Roll

Materials needed: a green and a purple crayon

Learning something new should get you charged up and ready to roll as you fill up with new information. Complete the organizer below to show how charged up and filled up with knowledge you are about today's topic.

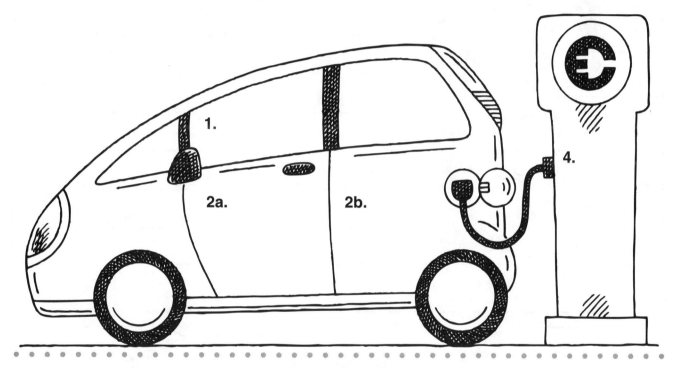

Directions: Complete each section of the graphic organizer.

1. What was the topic of the lesson?

2. **a.** Write one vocabulary word from the lesson.

   b. Write the definition of the word.

3. Color the car green if you feel great about the lesson. Color the car purple if you have questions about the lesson.

4. Write one good question about today's topic that could be used on a quiz. Be sure to include the answer.

I Heard It; I Saw It

Directions: Think about today's lesson. Write two facts about the topic that you heard during the lesson.

Then write or draw two examples or illustrations you saw and learned about during the lesson.

I heard _____

_____

_____

_____

_____

_____

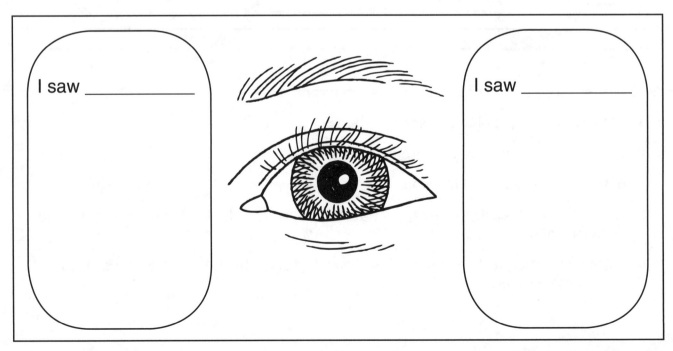

I saw _____   I saw _____

Name: _____

Did You Get the Point?

Directions: Think about today's topic or standard. Summarize the main points of the lesson in the arrows below.

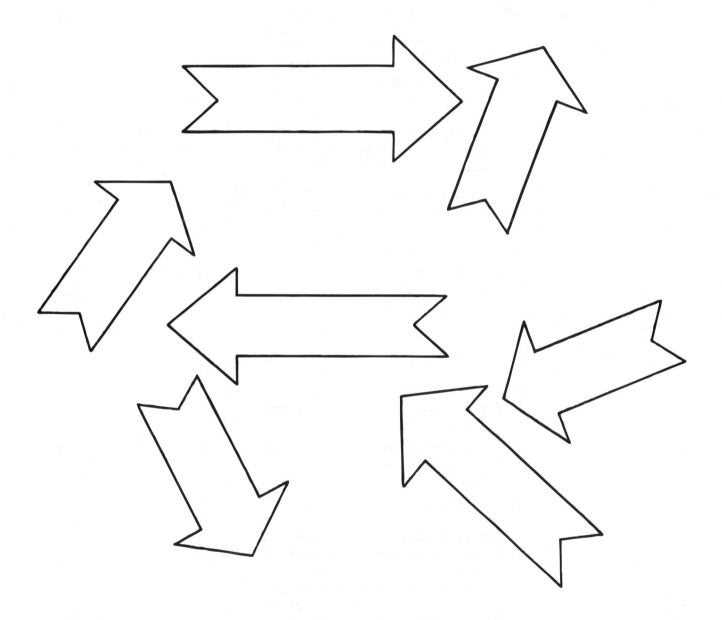

Circle your answer:

I understand the main point(s) of today's lesson.

I need more help with today's lesson.

Name: _____

A Real Exit Ticket

Materials needed: purple, red, green, and yellow crayons

Imagine you cannot complete your exit from class today until you can explain the lesson to the teacher. Complete the exit ticket below to prove you are good to go!

1. What was the topic of today's lesson?

_____

Color the **E** green if you know the answer.

2. List two important terms used with today's lesson.

   a. _____.

   b. _____.

Color the **X** yellow if you know what each term means.

3. Color the **I** purple if you understand today's lesson.

Color the **I** red if you need help with today's lesson.

4. **T** is the last letter of the word "exit" and the first letter of the word "teacher." Pretend you are the teacher and think of one great quiz question you could ask the class about today's lesson. Write the question and the answer beside the Exit sign.

Now hand your ticket to the real teacher...to find out if you are free to exit!

Name: _____

Four Squares

Directions: Complete each section of the organizer using the information you learned in today's lesson. Information can be written or illustrated.

Today's Lesson or Standard: _____

1. An example given in class of what we learned:	**2.** My own example of what we learned:
3. Two questions I still have about today's lesson:	**4.** Here is an example of how I will use the information I learned today outside of this class:

Name: _____

Recycle?

Directions: Think about today's lesson. Which parts of the lesson are things you will use again? Write the information on the labels of the cans in the recycling bin. You must write information on at least two cans. Remember to use examples from the lesson that you know you will use again (or recycle) outside of this classroom.

Hint: If you cannot think of two items for the recycling bin, write on the can labels and explain why you believe the information you learned will not be used again or recycled.

Something extra: When things are recycled, they are used again. Think of any topic or standard you have studied in this class. Which one have you recycled or used the most outside of school? Explain your answer.

_____

_____

_____

Name: _____

Loop De Loop

Directions: Complete each section of the graphic organizer.

1. a. Summarize today's lesson.

_____

_____

_____

b. On a scale of 1 to 5, how well do you feel you understand today's lesson? Write your

answer: _____

2. a. Is today's lesson similar to anything else you have studied?

_____

If yes, explain _____

_____

b. Where could you go to find out more information about today's topic?

_____

_____

3. Critique today's topic.

Hint: A critique can be positive or negative. You are not critiquing the teacher. You are critiquing the topic. For example, is this important to learn? If so, explain.

_____

_____

_____

Name: _____

A Baker's Dozen

Materials needed: crayons, any color

Directions: A baker's dozen is 13 rather than 12, so it's special. Show how special you are by showing how much you know about today's lesson. Below are 13 eggs. Write, draw, or give examples of 13 things you have learned about today's topic. Be sure to write the topic on the carton.

Don't know 13 things? Color any eggs you leave blank.

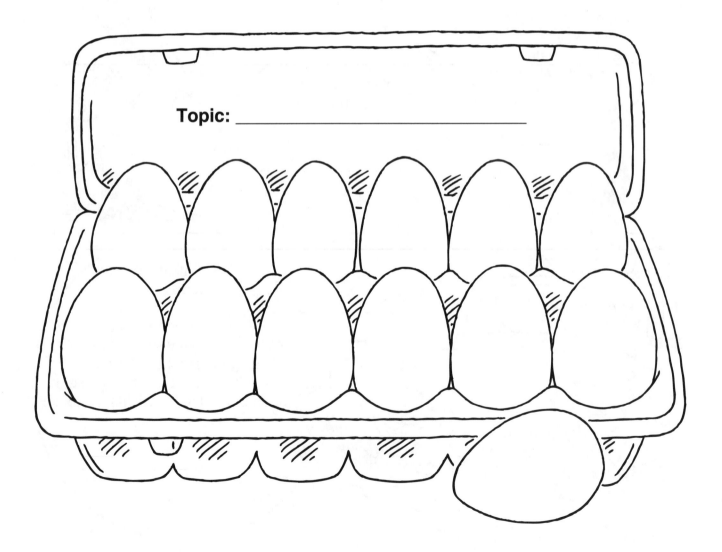

Topic: _____

Name: _____

Bow Tie Graph

Directions: Follow each direction and complete the graphic organizer below. Write the topic or standard of today's lesson inside the circle. Be sure to complete question 1 before the lesson begins. Finish question 2 after the lesson.

2. Write two new pieces of information you learned today.

Topic:

1. What did you already know about today's topic?

2.

1.

Name: _____

Into the Swing of It

Directions: Complete each part of the graphic organizer.

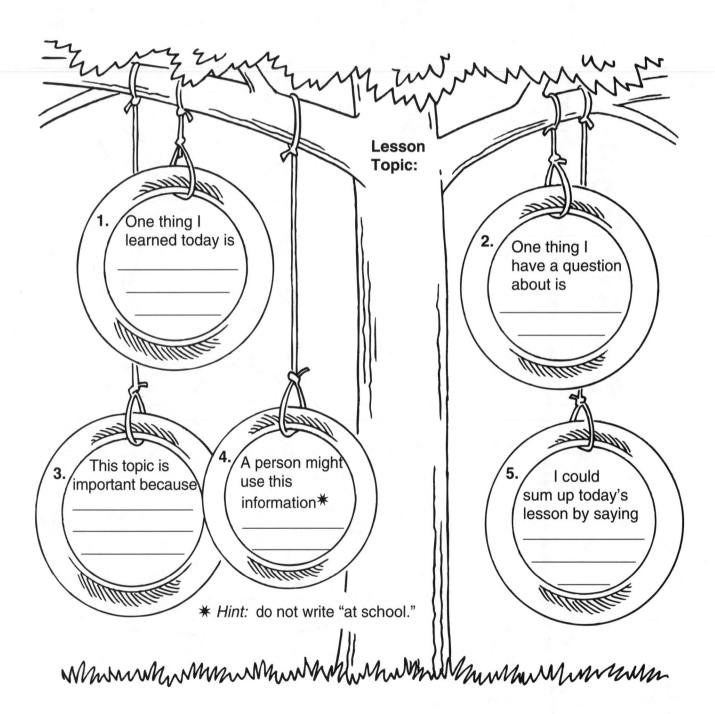

Lesson Topic:

1. One thing I learned today is _____ _____

2. One thing I have a question about is _____ _____

3. This topic is important because _____ _____

4. A person might use this information✲ _____ _____

5. I could sum up today's lesson by saying _____ _____

✲ *Hint:* do not write "at school."

Name: _____

3, 2, 1... Blast Off!

Directions: Complete each section of the graphic organizer.

1. Write the topic or standard of today's lesson to the right of the rocket.

2. On the base of the rocket, illustrate something you learned from today's lesson.

3. On the top of the rocket, write about what you have drawn.

Something extra: If you were teaching today's lesson, what is one thing you would teach

differently?_____.

What would you do to make this part of the lesson more easily understood?

_____.

Name: _____

Heart-to-Heart

When people have a "heart-to-heart," they have a detailed talk about a specific topic. Have a heart to heart about today's topic by completing the graphic organizer below.

Directions: Read and complete each section.

1. Explain why someone should learn about today's topic.

_____

_____

_____

_____

2. List two things you learned about today's topic.

_____

_____

_____

_____

3. Write two questions you have about today's topic.

_____

_____

_____

_____

4. Create an equation or illustration that shows something about today's topic.

Name: _____

Every Way

Directions: Complete the graphic organizer.

1. Illustrate something about the topic.

3. Explain how you could use the information you learned today outside of school.

1.
_____
_____
_____
_____
_____

2.
_____
_____
_____
_____

3.
_____
_____
_____
_____

4.
_____
_____
_____
_____

2. Sum up today's topic in three sentences or less.

4. Evaluate what is good or bad about today's lesson. Give at least two specific examples.

Name: _____

Five Major Points

Directions: Complete the graphic organizer below by writing the five major points about today's lesson or standard inside the points of the star. You can show examples to help explain any of your major points.

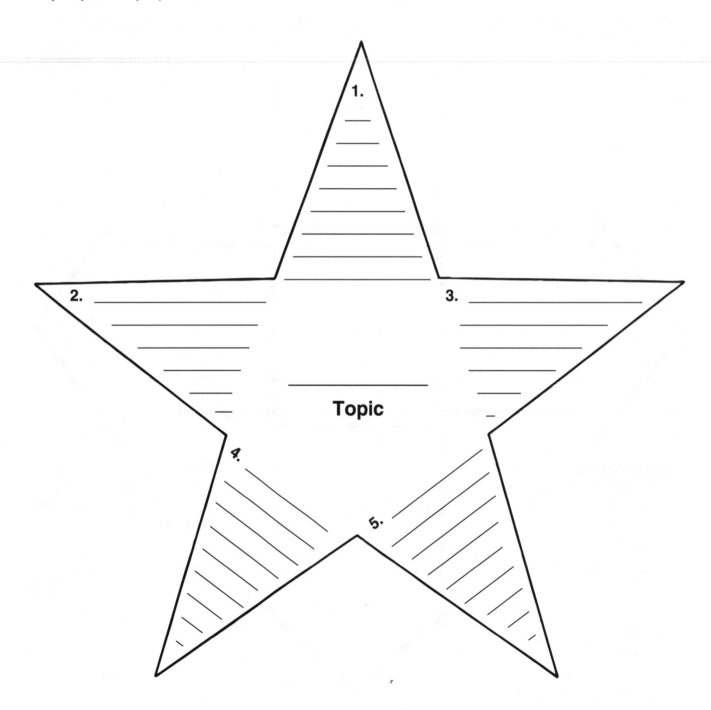

Name: _____

Take Four

Directions: Write the topic or standard on the line provided. Then take what you learned about today's topic or standard and give four different examples in each section of the graphic organizer

Example Topic: *Comma Rules*

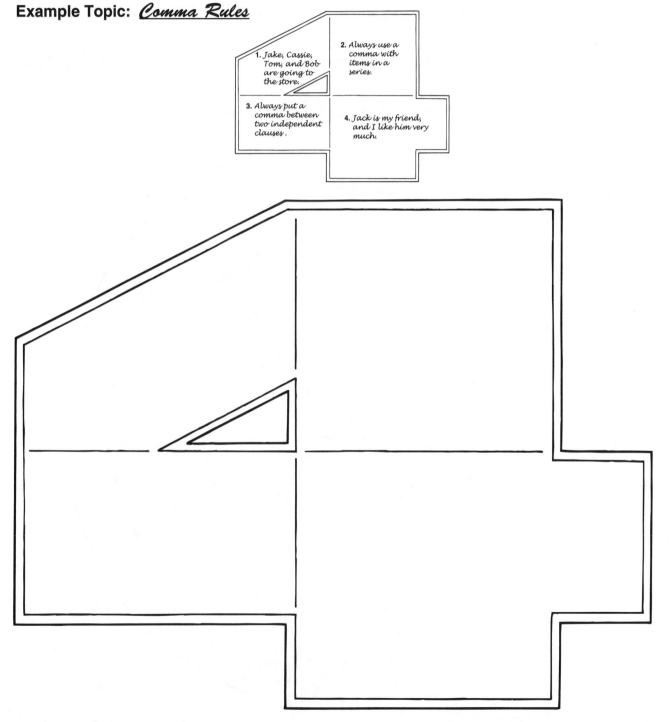

1. Jake, Cassie, Tom, and Bob are going to the store.

2. Always use a comma with items in a series.

3. Always put a comma between two independent clauses.

4. Jack is my friend, and I like him very much.

Write and Spin

Directions: Write what you learned about today's topic. Begin at the start line and spin the paper as needed to continue writing until you reach the end.

Because you listened well in class and took great notes, what's the challenge? You only have 120 seconds to complete the task. When you reach the center circle or the word "end," you are finished.

To keep the activity fun and fair, do not make the size of your letters larger than your regular writing style.

Wait for the teacher's signal to begin, and get ready to write and spin.

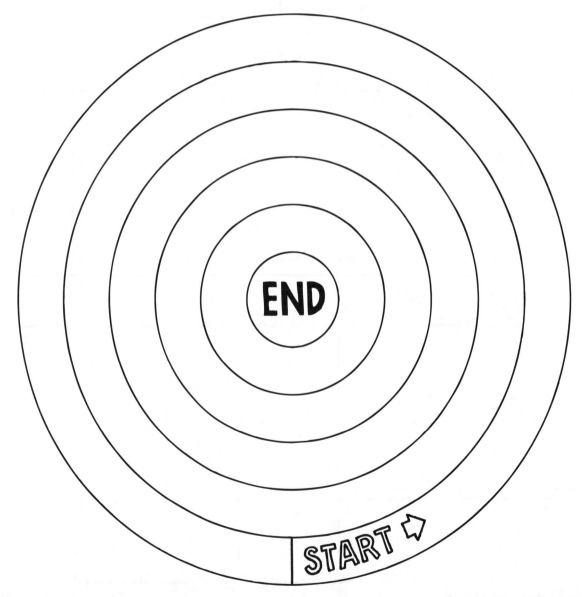

Name: _____

The Important Paragraph

Formative Assessment

A paragraph generally contains a topic sentence, supporting sentences, and a concluding sentence.

Use the paragraph outline below to help show what all you know about today's lesson.

Paragraph Outline:

Topic sentence _____ _____
Detail sentence _____ _____
Detail sentence _____ _____
Detail sentence _____ _____
Concluding sentence _____ _____

Name: _____

Caption Action

Directions: Create an illustration or a graph that shows information about today's topic or standard. Then write a caption of two to four sentences to explain the picture.

Caption:

_____

_____

_____

_____

Name: _____

Expressing the Lesson

Poetry is a type of writing that helps a writer express himself or herself in a way that is much different than writing prose. Use the poetry activity on page 40 to express what you know or still need to learn about today's lesson or standard. Use the example below to help get you started.

Finding a part of something bigger

Reducing to the simplest form

Add only if there's a common denominator

Can subtract, multiply, and divide in this form

Teacher, help me learn to simplify

I'll use fractions in life to compare numbers

Oh, I can see how I'll use this in life

Now, if I can just remember numerators are on top!

Name: _____

Expressing the Lesson *(cont.)*

Directions: Use the acrostic format to write a poem to explain the lesson or standard covered in class.

Write the main word or words of the topic vertically down the left side of the outlined section below. Each letter of the topic is capitalized and is the first letter of the word that begins each new line.

The words and lines created must refer to the topic listed vertically on the page. Use the example on page 39 for help. The lines of the poem can explain the topic or be used to ask questions.

Be sure to keep the first letters of each line written in a straight, vertical line so the word or words of the topic can be easily read.

First Letter

Name: _____

Class News

Directions: Complete each section of the class newspaper to explain today's topic or standard, or to ask any questions you might still have for the teacher about the lesson.

Section 1: Create a newspaper title that reflects the lesson. Include your name in the byline.

Section 2: Create a headline and article that explains and/or asks questions you have about the lesson.

Section 3: Draw a graph, illustration, or create an example that shows your knowledge of today's lesson. Include a caption to explain the information in the picture.

1.

_____

By _____

2.

_____

_____

_____

_____

_____

_____

_____

_____

_____

_____

_____

3.

_____

_____

_____

_____

Name: _____

5, 4, 3, 2, 1

Directions: Complete the activity below about today's lesson or standard.

A. List five facts from today's lesson. Use the back of the page if you need extra space.

1. _____

2. _____

3 _____

4. _____

5. _____

B. Write four reasons why today's lesson is important for you to learn. Do not include any reason related to testing.

1. _____

2. _____

3 _____

4. _____

C. Create three examples of your own to show you understand today's lesson. Use the back of the page if you need extra space.

1. _____

2. _____

3. _____

D. Compose two sentences that would summarize today's lesson to someone who was not present during the lesson.

1. _____

2. _____

E. Formulate one question you would like to ask the teacher about today's lesson.

1. _____

Name: _____

Formative Response

Explaining something you have learned requires a lot of skill. Show off your advanced skills in communication by explaining today's lesson or standard using the activity below.

Directions: Write a response for each section about today's lesson or standard.

1. State today's topic: _____

2. Compare today's lesson to another topic you have studied. List 2 ways they are similar. Use the back of the page if you need more space.

    a. _____

    b. _____

3. Expand on what you learned today by stating two ways today's lesson could be used outside of class.

    a. _____

    b. _____

4. Develop a definition, based on information you know, which would explain or define one of the main terms used in today's lesson.

    Term: _____

    Define: _____

5. Suggest one way the teacher might explain a concept taught in today's lesson that is different than the way the idea was taught today. Use the back of the page if you need more space.

    _____

    _____

    _____

I Have...Who Has?

Directions: Create your own "I Have...Who Has?" cards on page 45 using the information from academic terms you learned during today's lesson. Use the example below to help get you started.

Example Topic: Figurative Language

1.

I have the first card.

Who has a word that means the "repetition of a consonant sound at the beginning of each word"?

2.

I have **alliteration.**

Who has a word that means "words that share the same ending sound"?

3.

I have **rhyme.**

Who has a word that means "a word that stands for a noise or sound"?

4.

I have **onomatopoeia.**

Who has a word that means "giving living characteristics to nonliving things"?

5.

I have **personification.**

Who has a word that compares things using "like" or "as"?

6.

I have **simile.**

This is the last card.

Name: _____

I Have... Who Has? *(cont.)*

Directions: Create "I Have... Who Has?" cards using the templates below. All five cards should refer to vocabulary words or specific examples taught during today's lesson. The final card will not contain a definition. Use the example on page 44 to help get you started.

Lesson topic or standard: _____

1.
I have _____.
Who has _____
_____?

2.
I have _____.
Who has _____
_____?

3.
I have _____.
Who has _____
_____?

4.
I have _____.
Who has _____
_____?

5.
I have _____.
Who has _____
_____?

6.
I have _____.
Who has _____
_____?

Something extra: Want to impress your teacher and show how much you know about an entire unit of study? Create a class set of "I Have...Who Has?" cards by using index cards. Create at least one card for each student in the class. Be sure to have a beginning and ending card for the set you create and do include an answer key.

Name: _____

Completion Card

Directions: Complete each section about today's standard or topic.

1. Explain the skill.	**2.** Illustrate or show an original example.
3. Give an argument why today's lesson is a skill students need to learn.	**4.** Give an argument why today's lesson is not a skill students need to learn.

Name: _____

Analogies

An analogy makes an association or a comparison between items. For example, **day** is associated with the **sun** as **night** is associated with the **moon**. Analogies are often written in the following format:

> day: sun :: night: moon

> Day is to sun as night is to moon.

Part 1

Directions: Create three analogies using information from today's lesson.

Example:

Topic: Reconstruction after the Civil War

1. Lincoln : former :: Johnson : new
2. 13th amendment: freedom :: 14th : citizenship
3. Freedmen's Bureau : help :: carpetbagger : damage

1. _____ : _____ :: _____ : _____ :
2. _____ : _____ :: _____ : _____ :
3. _____ : _____ :: _____ : _____ :

• •

Part 2

Directions: Explain the relationship of each analogy created in Part 1. Use the back of the page if you need more space.

1. _____   2. _____

   _____   _____

   _____   _____

   _____   _____

3. _____

   _____

   _____

   _____

Name: _____

Trading Cards

There are many types of trading cards. Some are sold in packages with gum or other treats. Some are cards about favorite sports teams or favorite cartoon characters. People who collect trading cards generally have a lot of knowledge about the topic of the cards they collect. Show off your knowledge about today's lesson by creating a trading card of your own.

Directions: Use the space below to design the front and back of a trading card about today's topic or standard. Design an illustration for the front of the card that reflects information from the lesson. Use the reverse side of the card to list facts and ask a question about the topic.

Important facts:

_____

_____

_____

Wish I knew more about this:

_____

_____

_____

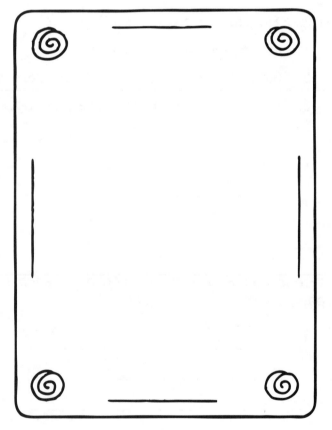

Name: _____

Dear...,

Directions: Use the piece of stationery below to write a letter to your teacher. Write about today's lesson. Be sure to include these three things in your letter.

1. Summarize the lesson in one to three sentences.

2. Explain why the skill is important to learn. (Do not use testing as a reason.)

Hint: You can also include other information in your letter.

Dear _____,

_____

_____

_____

_____

_____

_____

_____

_____

_____

_____

_____

Your student,

_____

Name: _____

Questions and Answers

Part 1

Directions: Think about what you have learned today. Now create three word-problem or essay-style questions that could be used to test other students' knowledge about today's lesson.

> 1.

> 2.

> 3.

Part 2

Directions: Write the answers to the problems you have created on the back of the page. Be sure to number your answers.

Name: _____

Seasonal Response

Most people have a favorite season. Think about which season you like best, and use the information to help you complete the formative assessment activity below.

Directions: Complete each section and compare today's topic or standard to your favorite season.

Today's topic or standard: _____

Favorite season: _____

1. List three words that describe your favorite season. _____

_____

2. Circle two of the three words listed in #1 and explain how these words could also describe today's topic.

   a. _____

       _____

   b. _____

       _____

3. What is one activity you can do during your favorite season?

_____

_____

4. What is one activity you can do outside of school with the standard or skill you learned today?

_____

5. Create an analogy comparing your favorite season to today's topic.

_____: _____: _____: _____

       (is to)   (as)   (is to)

Name: _____

All About You

Directions: Create an interview with... yourself! Create four questions about today's lesson or topic. You do not have to go far to find the responses. You answer your own questions on the lines provided.

1. Question:

_____

_____

Answer:

_____

_____

2. Question:

_____

_____

Answer:

_____

_____

3. Question:

_____

_____

Answer:

_____

_____

4. Question:

_____

_____

Answer:

_____

_____

Name: _____

Imagine a World Without...

Formative Assessment

Directions: Think about the lesson or skill that was taught today in class. Now imagine a world that no longer involved the information you learned. Write a short story below explaining what the world would be like if the information taught in today's lesson no longer existed.

Use the following lines to write about the experience.

A World Without _____

(today's topic or standard)

_____

_____

_____

_____

_____

_____

_____

_____

_____

_____

_____

_____

Name: _____

My Passport

A passport is a document that aids a person in traveling around the world. A good education is like a passport because it, too, has the ability to take you places in life.

Complete the passport below to be able to leave today's lesson and move on to your next subject, so you can continue your future travels and quest for knowledge.

Passport

The card that can take you places... just like a good education.

_____

Name of student traveler: _____

What topic or standard did you learn today on your quest for knowledge?

_____

List two important terms, formulas, etc. you learned during today's lesson.

a. _____

b. _____

How might someone in another country use the information you learned today? (Do not use testing as an example.)

_____

_____

What one part of the lesson would you send "packing" if you could? Explain.

_____

_____

_____

What one part of the lesson would you like to keep with you as you travel through life? Explain.

_____

_____

_____

Name: _____

For Sale

Directions: Create a newspaper advertisement on page 56 that sells today's topic. Be creative but also include the required information below:

• Explain the topic.

• Include any key terms or information.

• Give examples, illustrations, graphs, or samples if needed.

Example:

For Sale

Information about the United States in World War II and the bombing of Pearl Harbor

This information is vital to anyone who wishes to understand the memorial located at Pearl Harbor in Hawaii.

Seller will cover cost of shipping and handling on the following items:

· Photograph of the U.S. President, Franklin D. Roosevelt, president during the bombing of Pearl Harbor and most of World War II

· Autobiography of the life of a kamikaze pilot from Japan

· A map highlighting the route the Empire of Japan used before attacking the United States

If you order within 24 hours, you'll also receive for FREE the following terms and definitions engraved in jewelry made from genuine cubic zirconia:

· the years the war lasted for the United States: 1941–1945

· the names of the Axis powers: Japan, Italy, and Germany

Name: _____

For Sale *(cont.)*

Use the directions from page 55 and the space below to create a for-sale advertisement about the topic or standard you studied in class.

For Sale

This information is vital to anyone who...

Seller will cover cost of shipping and handling on the following items:

If you order within 24 hours, you'll also receive...

Name: _____

Where's the Information?

Directions: Use the space below to draw or write eight pictures, words, phrases, equations, etc. about today's lesson. Use the items to create a collage of information with very little white or blank space in between each item. Within the collage, also include examples that are not related to the lesson or skill being taught.

On the back of the page, explain what you have included in the picture that relates to today's lesson and explain the connection or importance of each item to what is being studied in class.

Finally, with the teacher's permission, exchange papers with a classmate. Try and find the items that are NOT related to today's lesson within each collage of information. Circle the items you find.

Check each other's papers for accuracy.

Name: _____

Scrambled Facts

Part 1

Directions: Create five scrambled facts about today's lesson. Write the answer to each scrambled fact on the back of the page. Facts should be easily understood but do not have to be written as complete sentences.

Example: Lesson topic or standard: <u>Commas</u>

between series. Use items commas a in
Answer: Use commas between items in a series.

Scrambled Facts:

a. _____

b. _____

c. _____

d. _____

e. _____

Part 2

When you are finished with Part 1, with your teacher's permission, exchange papers with another student in the class. Write the unscrambled facts from your partner's paper in Part 2 of the paper you are working on. Check each other's papers for accuracy.

Unscrambled Facts:

1. _____

2. _____

3 _____

4. _____

5. _____

Name: _____

The Red Effect

Materials needed: red pen or red colored pencil

Part 1

Directions: Think about today's lesson. How would you explain the skill taught in today's lesson to someone who was not in the class? Could you teach the lesson to someone who was absent?

In the space below or on another paper, write a summary of today's lesson, but you must include three examples in your summary that are actually false. Do not make these statements stand out in any way or look different from the rest of the summary that does contain accurate facts. If you run out of room, continue your summary on the back of this page.

Hint: In Part 2, you will exchange your paper with a partner to see if he or she can find your mistakes.

Example: Today's topic or standard: the planets

(There are twelve planets in our solar system.) Earth is the third planet from the sun. This distance is just right to sustain life, unlike (Mars, which is the closest planet to the Sun.) Earth is bordered by two planets, which aren't really near to us like many of our neighbors in our own neighborhoods; (these two neighboring planets are Venus and Jupiter.) Many of the planets get their names from Roman mythology. Venus is the only planet named after a female. An astronomer is someone who studies the planets and outer space.

Fictitious sections of statements have been circled.

```
Lesson Summary: _____

_____

_____

_____

_____
```

Part 2

Directions: When you are finished and with the teacher's approval, exchange papers with another student. Use a red pen and circle any information in the summary that is not true. Check each other's papers for accuracy. Be ready to explain your answer choices.

Name: _____

Creating Couplets

Directions: With the teacher's help, divide into groups of two. (If needed, there can be a group of three.) Students working in groups will each write answers on their own sheets of paper although answers can be the same.

With the help of your partner, create couplets (two lines of poetry which rhyme) about today's topic. Be sure to include major points that were covered. You can also include questions that you or your partner may still have about the lesson.

Example:

Quotation Marks

Use this important punctuation mark

To know who's talking, so you're not in the dark

Place them around exactly what was said

So you'll know if the words were Marcia's, Ina's, or even Ted's

Use Q.M.'s around the titles of poems

But do we use them around book titles in our homes?

Use the space below to create your rhyming verses. Use the back of the page if you need more space. Remember, each set of two lines needs to rhyme.

Name: _____

Five Questions and Answers

Part 1

Directions: Write five questions about today's lesson. Write the answer to each question on the back of this page.

1. _____

2. _____

3 _____

4. _____

5. _____

Part 2

Directions: With the teacher's permission, and once everyone in the class is finished, rotate throughout the classroom and ask five different students to answer at least one of the questions in Part 1.

Record the answers below.

1. _____

2. _____

3 _____

4. _____

5. _____

Part 3

Directions: Draw a star beside the answers you know are correct. Draw a triangle by the answers you believe are incorrect. Be ready to explain to the teacher why you believe an answer is incorrect.

Name: _____

All I Got Was This Shirt

Directions: There are T-shirts everywhere with clever sayings or funny expressions. With the help of the teacher, the class will divide into small groups of three to four students. Use the space below to design a T-shirt where the writing shows what your group knows about today's lesson topic or standard.

Name: _____

Five

Directions: With the teacher's help, the class will divide into groups of five. (If needed, some groups may be slightly larger or smaller.) Each member of the group will complete his or her own worksheet; but the group should offer suggestions and help each other as needed.

With help from the entire group, complete each of the five sections. Be sure to share ideas with the members of your group so everyone can complete each section.

1. List five adjectives that describe today's lesson or standard.

_____

_____

_____

_____

_____

_____

_____

2. List five examples of how today's skill could be used outside of school.

_____

_____

_____

_____

_____

_____

_____

5. List five questions you would like to ask the teacher about today's lesson.

_____

_____

_____

_____

_____

3. List five facts from the lesson.

_____

_____

_____

_____

_____

_____

_____

_____

4. List the five most important points from today's lesson.

_____

_____

_____

_____

_____

_____

_____

Name: _____

Clues

Part 1

Directions: Use the space below to create four three-tiered statements about today's topic. Each statement is a clue leading to the final answer. Use the example to help guide you in creating your own.

Example:

Lesson topic: States of Matter

1. Water is one.

2. It conforms to the shape of the container where it is kept.

3. Not a solid.

Answer: liquid

Lesson topic: _____

A.

1. _____

2. _____

3. _____

Answer: _____

C.

1. _____

2. _____

3. _____

Answer: _____

B.

1. _____

2. _____

3. _____

Answer: _____

D.

1. _____

2. _____

3. _____

Answer: _____

Once you have finished Part 1, you are ready for Part 2 on page 65.

Name: _____

Clues (cont.)

Part 2

Directions: With the help of the teacher, divide into small groups of three to four students.

Each member of the group will take a turn reading his or her statements out loud from page 64. The reader should read one statement and then pause to see if someone in the group can guess the answer before moving to the next clue. If no one can guess the answer after all the clues have been given, the student who created the question should read the answer to the group. Students in the group should take turns asking questions of each other until all questions have been completed.

With the teacher's permission, the group can have a competition against other groups in the class by assigning point values to each clue.

Points can be assigned as follows:

- If any of the students in the group can guess the answer with only the first clue given, the group gets 15 points for that question.

- If the members of the group answer correctly on the second clue, the group gets 10 points.

- If the members of the group answer correctly on the third clue, the group gets 5 points.

- If no one can guess the answer, the student who created the question will explain the answer to the group. If the group disagrees with the answer, no points will be assigned, but the teacher should be consulted to see if the statements or answer is written incorrectly. All students should be sure to create statements and answers that are accurate about the lesson since no points can be given to poorly constructed clues.

- Because some groups may not be equal in size, if keeping score, groups should only compete against groups with the same number of students. If this is not possible, the teacher can adjust the number of questions.

  If needed, use another sheet of paper to help keep score.

Name: _____

At the Tip of My Fingers

Directions: Use the space below to complete the following activity.

Work with another student and help each other trace the outline of each person's hand. (Only trace one hand.) On the piece of paper, write the topic of today's lesson on the palm of your hand. Write one fact you learned about today's lesson on one of the traced fingers. Sign your name after your written fact. Then walk around the room and find four different students to complete facts on each remaining traced finger. Each student must sign his or her name. No facts can be repeated. If a student cannot respond with a different fact than the ones which have already been written, have the student sign his or her name in the palm of the hand, and move on to another student.

Name: _____

Five Minutes

Part 1

Directions: Think about today's lesson or standard. You have five minutes to write down as much as you can about today's lesson. The information does not have to be written in complete sentences; however, the information must be accurate. If more space is needed, use the back of this page.

For example:

Food and shelter are needed. (Not enough information—needed for what?)

Living things need food and shelter. (Enough information is given—who needs food and shelter is identified.)

1. _____   2. _____

   _____   _____

3. _____   4. _____

   _____   _____

5. _____   6. _____

   _____   _____

7. _____

   _____

Part 2

Directions: When everyone has finished Part 1, wait for the teacher's instruction to continue. You will have five minutes to walk around the classroom and compare your information to that of your classmates. For each statement you have that is the same or similar to someone else's information, draw a star beside the number. For example, if two people have the same information you have on #2, draw two stars beside the number.

When the five minutes are complete, count the total number of stars you have and write the number on the line below. The teacher will check to see who has the most stars. The student who has the most stars is the five-minute champion for listening to the lesson and remembering important facts so well.

Total: _____

Name: _____

Take the Cake

Wait for the teacher's directions. The teacher will divide the students into small groups of three to four students. Once you are assigned a group, complete the task below.

Directions: Work with your group to come up with a cupcake design for the cupcake picture on page 69 that reflects how much you know about today's lesson. Each person in the group must decorate his or her own cupcake, but the group should offer suggestions and help each other as needed. Cupcakes can all be decorated alike if the group chooses to use the same designs. Remember: every design must be a part of today's lesson. Be ready to explain the various designs and their meanings as the teacher looks at each group's creations.

Use the example below to help get you started.

Example:

Lesson Topic: <u>The Great Depression</u>

Name: _____

Take the Cake *cont.*

Materials needed: crayons, markers, or colored pencils

Follow the directions on page 68 to complete the picture below.

Lesson Topic: _____

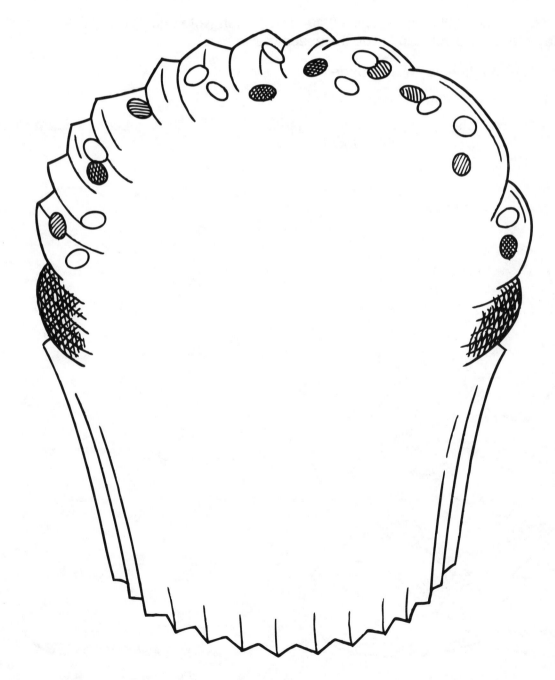

Name: _____

It's Super!

Superheroes have amazing powers. Many are known for their super strength or super speed, but the superhero below is known for his super mind. Where does he get all his power from, you ask? Why, you, of course! Fill the superhero's thoughts with facts from today's lesson to help create the best superhero of all... Super-Smart Student!

Part 1

Directions: Think about today's topic or standard. Then write and/or illustrate as many facts from today's lesson as you can inside the space drawn below.

List ten facts—your hero is an A+, super-smart student!

List nine to five facts—your hero is a good student!

List less than five facts—your hero needs to get help from the super teacher to learn
more about today's topic

Name: _____

It's Super! *(cont.)*

Materials needed: yellow crayon

Part 2

Directions: Wait for the teacher's instructions to continue. When everyone in the class has finished and the teacher gives the signal to begin, walk around with your superhero picture and see what other students have written for their answers. If any of your answers are similar to or exactly the same as the other students' answers, highlight the information on your page with a yellow crayon. Information that is unique to your superhero will not be highlighted. You will have five minutes to look at as many papers as you can.

Once five minutes are completed, return to your seat and wait for the teacher to read the directions to Part 3.

Part 3

Directions: Choose one of the facts you have highlighted. In the space below, design a logo for the superhero's costume using the information from one highlighted fact. Use the lines below to write an explanation about the logo.

Name: _____

Lucky Clovers

Directions: Use the four-leaf clover below to show what you know about today's lesson or standard. Wait for the teacher to divide the class into groups of three to four students. With the help of the members of the group, write what you know about today's lesson or standard on the lines inside the clover. Each student in the group must complete his or her own clover; however, information can be the same.

Name: _____

Bright Ideas

With the help of the teacher, get in small groups of two to three students. Then complete each section below.

Part 1

Directions: Discuss the topic of today's lesson with the members of the group. List three bright ideas from the lesson on the three light bulbs below. Include any examples or details that will help explain your choices.

Part 2

Directions: Discuss with the group anything from the lesson about which you wish you knew more or could receive additional instruction. Write the group's wishes on each candle.

Something extra: On the back of this page, share a bright idea your group has for teaching the standard in today's lesson.

Name: _____

The Group Answers

Directions: Make one copy of this page. Then use the space below to create a list of at least 10 true-or-false questions students should be able to correctly answer about a lesson you have taught. Be sure to include answers for each question. Then make enough copies of page 75 for each student in the class. Use the statements created on this page to complete the formative assessment activity on page 75.

1. _____

   Answer: _____

2. _____

   Answer: _____

3. _____

   Answer: _____

4. _____

   Answer: _____

5. _____

   Answer: _____

6. _____

   Answer: _____

7. _____

   Answer: _____

8. _____

   Answer: _____

9. _____

   Answer: _____

10. _____

   Answer: _____

Name: _____

The Group Answers (cont.)

Materials needed: scissors

Directions: Cut out each rectangle below. Stand up beside your desk and listen as the teacher reads out loud questions about today's topic. If the answer to the question is "true," hold the **True** card straight out in front of you. If the answer is "false," hold the **False** card above your head.

Once the teacher gives the correct answer, place your hands behind your back and wait to answer the next question. In between questions, cards can be held in your hands or placed on your desk until you need them.

True

False

Name: _____

No Monkeying Around

Part 1

Directions: Write facts, examples, illustrations, etc., that you understand from today's lesson on each monkey. Write things on the banana peel about the lesson that you feel might slip you up. You do not have to write information on each picture, but do complete as many pictures as possible.

Part 2

Directions: When everyone has finished, and with the teacher's permission, move around the room and ask students in the class to help explain any questions you have written on the banana peels. Then ask the teacher for help on any questions you still need answered.

Once you understand a question, draw a circle around each banana peel to show this information will no longer slip you up about today's topic.

Student with a Blog

Directions: Use the space below to create a blog. What's a blog? A blog is usually created as a website with information that includes a person's opinions or observations about specific topics.

Use the space below to write your own questions, comments, examples, and/or illustrations about today's lesson or standard. Write the example as if you were actually going to create a blog that could be viewed by others.

Creating a blog can be a fun way to share your thoughts and opinions, and there are various free sites that can be used. However, you should never create a blog without permission.

Say It With Music

Directions: With the teacher's permission, search the Web using school-appropriate sites only to find lyrics and song titles that remind you of either things you learned from the lesson or the things you didn't understand. Write down the titles and an explanation for each choice. If you need more space, use the back of this worksheet. Writing the artist associated with each song is optional.

Some sections can remain blank.

Example:

Song Title: "We Are Never, Ever Getting Back Together" by Taylor Swift because we studied magnets, and poles on magnets repel and can never get together.

Things I Understand	**Things I Do Not Understand**
Song Title: _____	Song Title: _____
because _____	because _____
_____	_____
_____	_____
_____	_____
Song Title: _____	Song Title: _____
because _____	because _____
_____	_____
_____	_____
_____	_____
Song Title: _____	Song Title: _____
because _____	because _____
_____	_____
_____	_____
_____	_____

Projection Templates #1

Formative Assessment

Directions: Choose from the following templates to use as a formative assessment. Save time and copies by projecting the formative assessment you choose onto an interactive whiteboard, or use a document camera to show the assessment to the class if your classroom does not have an interactive board. Students can answer using the interactive whiteboard (if available), verbally, or on their own paper. The assessment can, of course, be copied for each student if no technology is available.

Formative Assessment

Template #1

1. Summarize the lesson in one to two sentences.

   _____

   _____

   _____

   _____

2. Explain how this skill will be used with previous learning. If you cannot think of a way the skill is connected to previous learning, explain how you might use the skill outside of school.

   _____

   _____

   _____

3. On a scale of one to five stars, with five stars being the best, circle your rating of today's lesson.

   ☆ ☆ ☆ ☆ ☆

Formative Assessment

Template #2

1. List 3 major terms from today's lesson.

   a. _____

   b. _____

   c. _____

2. Give two examples, equations, illustrations, etc. about today's skill.

   a. _____

   _____

   b. _____

   _____

3. Circle the picture below which best reflects your understanding of the lesson.

Projection Templates #2

formative
Assessment

Directions: Choose from the following templates for a formative assessment. Create a copy of the template. Next, make the assessment more specific to a standard by adding information to the template. Be sure to assess only those skills that are appropriate for showing whether students have mastered the standard. Use the content-specific assessment as an interactive whiteboard assignment, or use a document camera to display the adapted copy of the assessment to the class. Using this method will often save both time and copies while still accurately checking for students' understanding of the lesson.

A. Define the following terms used in today's lesson.

1. _____   2. _____

B. Design an original example of a skill from today's lesson.

For example, here is one you were shown in class. Now create your own:

C. Summarize what you learned from today's lesson in three sentences or less. The first sentence has been done for you.

_____

_____

A. Which set of words best describes the topic of today's lesson?

1. _____   2. _____

B. Explain two ways today's skill can be used outside of school.

Here is one idea: _____

1. _____   2. _____

C. Decide if the following statement is true or false in regards to today's lesson. Then explain your answer.

_____

This statement is _____ because _____